BECOME A FREELANCE SALES AGENT IN THE UK

Terry James
and
David Boden

© 2006 by Terry James
Revised 2019

All rights reserved. No part of this work may be reproduced, or stored in an information retrieval system, (except for short extracts for the purpose of review), without the express permission of the author given in writing.

Note: The material contained in this book is set out in good faith for general guidance and the author cannot accept liability for any loss or expense incurred as the result of relying in any particular circumstances on statement made in this book. The laws and regulations are complex and changing. Readers of the book should always check the current position with the relevant authorities before acting.

Publisher: Terry James
        X L Systems
        3 Greenfields Close
        Drakes Broughton
        Pershore
        Worcs. WR10 2BD
        UK

Contents

	Foreword	7
	Preface	8
1	**Becoming a sales agent**	**10**
	What is a sales agent?	11
	Will I make a sales agent?	11
	Are their age limits?	13
	How fit do I have to be?	13
	What are the rewards?	13
	What are the risks?	14
	Questions and answers	15
	Case studies	16
	Why the principal needs you	**18**
	Your cost benefit	18
	Bringing in the principal a new customer base	19
	9Assisting product biased companies	19
	Reducing your disadvantages	20
	Working in traditional 'sales agent' industries.	22
	Questions and answers	22
	Case studies	22

	How to set up as a sales agent	**25**
	Preparing a business plan	25
	Finance and where to get it	26
	Deciding your territory	26
	Working from home	27
	Your legal status	27
	Managing Tax and VAT	28
	HMRC Definition of Self Employed	28
	Using an accountant	29
	The VAT Position	29
	Questions and answers	30
	Looking for your first agencies	**32**
	Where to look for sales agencies	32
	Assessing a good agency	32
	How many agencies should you hold	33
	Specialising in a market sector	33
	Approaching a prospective agency	33
	Producing an agency profile	34
	Questions and answers	35
	Case studies	36
5	**Selling yourself to the principal**	**37**
	Choosing the meeting venue	37
	What will the principal be looking for	37
	What should you be looking for	38
	Asking the right questions	40
	Managing the interview	40
	Managing the follow up	40
	Questions and answers	41
	Case studies	41

6	**Negotiating the formal agreement**	**43**
	Requesting an agreement	43
	The Commercial Agents Regulations (1993)	43
	The elements of the agreement	44
	If the agreement is breached	44
	Questions and answers	45
	Case studies	45

7	**Carrying out checks on the principal**	**47**
	Checking with your bank	47
	Using a credit information agency	47
	Companies House Website	47
	Identifying a risky Principal	47
	Speak to his existing Agents	48
	Questions and answers	48
	Case studies	49

8	**Running your agency**	**51**
	Buying and running a car	51
	Invoicing and chasing your commission	52
	Managing your finances	52
	Communication with your principals	53
	The importance of journey planning	53
	Protecting your legal rights	54
	Questions and answers	54
	Case studies	55

9	**Sales Agents and the Digital Age**	**57**
	How technology helps your business	57
	Dealing with Principals who sell via websites	57

	Using SocialMedia	58
10	**Developing your customer base**	**60**
	The agents independent role	60
	Keeping your customers informed	60
	Promoting your full range	61
	Helping your principal get paid	61
	Questions and answers	63
	Case studies	63
11	**Looking ahead**	**66**
	Increasing the geographical area	66
	Expanding your product base	66
	Taking on sub-agents	67
	Employing salespeople yourself	67
	Taking on overseas agencies	67
	Questions and answers	68
	Case studies	69

Appendix 1: Summary of Commercial Agents Regulations — 67

Appendix 2: A typical agency agreement — 75

Useful Addresses & Links — 77

FOREWORD

Sales agency work is highly specialised, and is an incredibly valuable and worthwhile pursuit. As the UK's main Sales Agent Register, we are delighted that you are buying this book! It means you are either seriously considering becoming a sales agent, or that you wish to improve your performance as a sales agents.

The UK needs more professional sales agents. Demand out-strips supply which is great news for you! You will have quite some choice of agency opportunities, and the opportunity to earn a very good income once you have established yourself with a network of customers and a portfolio of good products or services.

The latter is the mission of AgentBase - to provide you with the best stream of agency opportunities possible. Something we have been doing since 1993. Now thousands of UK sales agents regularly use the AgentBase magazine and website to find new agency opportunities. And it's all completely free of charge.

This is how we met the author of this book, Terry James. Terry is one of our long-standing members, and now deservedly retired. He is not an academic that decided to research a subject and write a book. He was out there, practicing what he preaches, for many many years. And as they say, what he doesn't know about agency work probably isn't worth knowing!

Recently the book has been revised with the assistance of a co-author, David Boden, who is an experienced and currently active sales agent. His ongoing experience has been invaluable in bringing the book up to date with current technology and practices.

This is, to our knowledge, the only book *for* sales agents written *by* sales agents, and as such is *the* authoritative reference point for all aspiring agents. I welcome you to agency work, and recommend this book most sincerely.

Paul G Brown

Founder and MD

AgentBase UK Sales Agent Register

www.agentbase.co.uk

PREFACE

Terry James: I became a freelance sales agent by accident, having risen to management status in sales and having been through a spate of redundancies, it was a case of 'the higher you rise the further you fall'. I got fed up with my fate being in the hands of others.

In searching for a solution to this problem, my thoughts naturally turned towards self employment. Having just reared a family my capital was very limited so starting my own company making or leasing out widgets and so forth was out of the question. An evaluation of my skills showed that my main experience lay in my lifetime experience in sales. But how was I to captalise on these skills without working for someone else?

A chance occurrence happened at this point. A previous colleague revealed that his company were seeking a sales agent in my area. As I was unemployed at the time I had nothing to lose by attending the interview. I was most impressed by the company and its products and was offered the agency.

Realising that it would take some time to get established, cover my expenses and make a profit, I set myself an extremely tight budget. I arranged a small overdraft with my bank and accepted the agency. As luck would have it I walked into a major order for the product almost immediately and was hooked on becoming a sales agent.

That was some fifteen years ago. I wish I could say it has been easy all the way but it has not. There have been good and bad times but that is true of life in general. I am not earning a fortune but I have something I prize above all else, my independence. I am now out of the rat race. I am not judged by whether my face fits into an organization or how I get on with the boss. I am judged by how much I sell. If I don't sell I don't eat. It is as simple as that.

I could earn considerably more if I worked harder but, approaching retirement age, I am starting to wind down. That is why I wanted to write this book, to pass on some of my experience to anybody who is thinking of becoming a freelance sales agent but is afraid of the unknown.

David Boden: My route to being a self-employed agent was similar to Terry James and I'm sure that both our stories resonate with many UK sales agents who have entered the world of sales agents in a similar way.

I became a self-employed sales agent thanks to a series of management changes within the group of companies I worked for, due to structural changes within the group my sales management role was diminishing and I was offered a number of options within the same group, including the opportunity to be a sales agent with a 5 year contract and as they say: "the rest is history"

Although I had the advantage of a contractual arrangement with my forma employer I still needed to deliver the sales to meet my obligations under the terms of the contract. But like many self-employed sales agents I had worked as a salaried employee within the sales environment for many years, in my case almost 30 years and during that time gained experience, knowledge and contacts.

Despite a contract, experience, knowledge and contacts I still needed finance to see me through the first few months and to purchase a car, mobile phone and computer. The majority of my financing came from my Bank, leasing agreements and savings, all supported by a good personal credit rating.

I was now ready to strike out on my own; it was both scary and exciting at the same time, but armed with a solid business plan and the determination to succeed as a freelance sales agent. That was over 8 years ago and I can say in all honesty despite the many ups and downs it was one of the best business decisions I have ever made, particularly as I have added complimentary agencies to my portfolio and diversified into other business ventures, this would have been impossible as an employee.

I see my sales agency as a continuation of my overall sales career, but the biggest difference is complete independence and freedom to make decisions that will benefit me rather than a board of directors or shareholders. During the past 8 years I have learnt to manage my time and genuinely developed a good work/life balance by working hard to maximise income and taking time off for leisure and holidays.

If you are considering a life as an independent sales agent, but you're fearful of the unknown I would suggest that you firstly read this book and secondly create a list of positives and negatives, if the positives outweigh the negatives then start building your new life as independent self-employed sales agent, I did and I only have one regret, that I didn't do it sooner.

Chapter 1

BECOMING A SALES AGENT.

WHAT IS A SALES AGENT?

A sales agent is a freelance, self employed sales person who works, usually alone, for perhaps several, non-competing, companies and obtains orders for those companies and is paid a commission on those orders. Each arrangement with each company is usually referred to as an agency. A sales agent sometimes describes the company he is working for as his principal. Sometimes a retainer is paid to the sales agent but this usually comes with strings attached.

He or she, usually works in a specific area of industry or commerce and usually within geographical limits. There are no limits to the types of industry and commerce where sales agents are found. Many companies use teams of sales agents to get national coverage and some companies use a mixture of employed salespeople and sales agents.

The sales agent is playing an ever increasing role in UK business. Many companies are looking hard at their costs and realising the real benefits of placing their sales efforts in the hands of the ever increasing number of competent and professional sales agents that are available today. In the United States, Europe and many other parts of the world, due to the large areas involved, the use of sales agents is quite normal. Normally only the major companies in these countries employ their own salesmen.

Sales agent or distributor, the difference?

There is a possible misunderstanding in the difference between a sales agent and a distributor.

The function of a distributor.

- purchases and holds stock
- solicits orders
- delivers the orders
- invoices the goods or service
- takes the credit risk
- makes a profit on the transaction

The function of a sales agent.

- solicits orders
- passes orders to the principle
- earns an agreed commission on those orders

Most Sales Agents consider themselves to be at the pinnacle of their sales career. They rely on their professionalism, salesmanship and customer relationships to earn their living. In return it is theoretically possible to enjoy an income far in excess of that usually earned by a company salesperson. The only limit to the size of their earnings is the amount of time, effort and salesmanship they put in. Not for them the petty squabbles, rivalry and jealousy that arise when such earnings are within a company structure.

Apart from the potential earnings the satisfaction derived from being the boss and running the company <u>their way</u> must be taken into account.

An inexpensive way of being your own boss.

Becoming a freelance sales agent is probably one of the least expensive and easiest routes for someone, with some sales experience, to having their own business. If you have a telephone, a computer, a car or access to some form of public transport and are reasonably competent at selling you can become a successful sales agent with all the pride, independence and earnings that are part of that success.

Remember, once you become a sales agent you will never ever become redundant. Principals may go bankrupt, or cease working with agents but you, wisely working for a range of principals, can carry on and replace the failed principal with your own choice in your own time.

WILL I MAKE A SALES AGENT?

The first and most important requirement for success as a sales agent is some sales experience. It is very difficult trying to cope with the inevitable mistakes made whilst learning to sell and, at the same time, trying to earn a living purely on how much you can sell.

Lots of companies use inexperienced people as employed salespeople on the basis that they have demonstrated some potential, they can train them into their own sales methods and they come relatively cheaply. The benefit to the inexperienced salesperson is that they make their mistakes and learn their craft at someone else's expense.

Self-discipline, it's your time and money.

Self-discipline is an essential quality. It is easy to find an excuse for not going out to call on prospective customers and spend time at home on various administrative jobs. That way eventually spells disaster.

Be prepared to.

- maximise your time with customers
- spends some spare time on administration
- be self-motivating
- not turn colds into flu
- set your own targets

Persistence and tenacity are other requirements. The going will get hard at times, especially while you are building the agency up. The ability to fight back after a major set-back is a necessary requirement for a sales agent. Set-backs come in varying ways, the failure of a principal, the loss of a large order or customer. When this happens you do not have the luxury of blaming others and still taking home a salary. You have to get out there and replace that lost income, with a smile on your face.

Most setbacks come in the early stages of your career as a sales agent. Experience teaches you how to avoid the most common causes of disappointments but they will always be there.

Doing it your way.

To some people it comes as a culture shock not to have colleagues around them to discuss matters regarding daily business life. To a certain extent you will have to become a loner but, as will be shown later, it is not a completely lonely life.

Making decisions alone will become second nature to you. You will make good and bad decisions. Luckily those decisions are yours and you can only blame yourself if it is a bad decision.

Make a decision before the money runs out.

The lack of initial financial pressure is very helpful in the first stages of becoming a sales agent. The need to earn and earn extremely quickly can cause problems in the initial period. If you are relying on redundancy money or other finance to tide you over the lean first months of setting up an agency, make the decision before the finance is exhausted.

Everybody has seen the results of salespeople that have to get the order there and then. They look desperate and it shows. The sales agent must have time to build customer confidence in him and the several product ranges he sells. This route usually leads to greater sales than can be achieved by a company salesperson who is just offering one product range.

ARE THERE AGE LIMITS?

The selling profession has no age barriers so becoming a sales agent follows this rule. It has the further advantage that sales agents sometimes carry on till a ripe old age. In salaried selling jobs an employer sometimes chooses younger salespeople because he can mould them to his liking and they probably come cheaper or work faster. With a sales agent the principal is not paying you for how many calls you put in or how hard you work, he is paying you for the orders you bring in. It matters not to him whether you are 20 or 90 years old, he still pays the same commission.

It is a fact that many agents carry on working for many years after the normal retirement age even if they do not need the money. They might cut down the number of agencies held or the distances travelled but they find it is a way of life they cannot completely give up. Sometimes it is the lack of a decent pension that prompts them to carry on working.

HOW FIT DO I HAVE TO BE?

Obviously the fitter you are the better you will be able to carry out your major function, contacting customers and obtaining orders. Nevertheless there are many agents that are successful despite medical problems that would probably deter their employment as a paid salesman.

Do tell any prospective principal of your condition and how you aim to get round it from the outset. If you can demonstrate a positive attitude towards your disorder and show him that your sales will not be affected overall, it should not go against you. They will respect your frankness.

WHAT ARE THE REWARDS?

Before you can make this decision you must get some information on the average amount of commission normally paid in your chosen area of operation. Commissions vary enormously but do tend towards the general rule that if there is much easy and quick repeat business to be had then the commission rate is lower than, at the other end of the scale, where the sale is a one off and may take many months, even years to bear fruit.

The commission rates also vary widely within any particular industry. However, in general they will tend average out at around 10%. If you have been working as a salesman in the industry where you intend to become a sales agent, as a quick calculation, take an estimated possible yearly turnover and 10% of that, your commission will be your theoretical nett income less, of course, your expenses which are dealt with later.

The income tax benefit.

A major advantage of being self-employed is in the system of taxation. Generally speaking the allowance for expenses are far more generous than with an employed person.

The tax benefits include

- only being taxed on the actual profits made
- wholly business expenses are tax deductible
- pension payments are tax deductible
- losses can be carried forward to a new tax year
- assets such as cars have a depreciation allowance

Nevertheless estimating your income in the early days is extremely difficult and not an exact art. It is easier to estimate your running expenses on a monthly basis, then add your estimate how much you need to live on as a minimum. This figure represents your needed income derived from sales at, say, 10% commission.

Do not forget that your first months income from sales will probably be nil and should increase from that point. You must set yourself some targets for sales, especially in the early months, as they are pointers towards your ultimate goal of paying your expenses, taking a wage and making a profit on top. Do not expect to make a profit in the first few months.

WHAT ARE THE RISKS?

The major way of minimising risk is, like the insurance companies, spreading the risks. Most sales agents represent several, non-competing companies, sometimes in the same Market area and sometimes spreading the risk even further by taking agencies on in different Market areas. In this way, even if an agency should not work out as you hoped for whatever reason, there are other agencies to fall back on.

The single agency lure.

A major potential pitfall is to concentrate on one agency only. It may be that their service or product is easy to sell and you can make an easy income from them to the detriment of any other agencies you hold.

Consider the following

- company policies towards agents do change
- try to have short, medium and long term income
- make sure your principals know you have other agencies.
- be prepared to weed out non-earning agencies

It is not uncommon for sales agents to build a company's sales up to a point where it is cheaper to pay an employed salesperson rather than pay extremely large commission cheques. The Commercial Agents Regulations 1993 can qualify you for compensation or indemnity should this occur.

Another strategy is to spread your agencies over short, medium and long term sales. Too much of either type can lead to risks. For example, short term business is usually quick selling, quick return and highly competitive. If your short term business principal becomes uncompetitive you have already laid down medium and long term strategies which give you time to await his return to competitiveness without losing your livelihood. At the other extreme too much reliance on long term business can lead to large gaps in your income and disappointment when that order you have been working on for many months is cancelled.

Most realistic principles will acknowledge your desire to work for other principals as well as them. Many of them could not realistically expect you to earn a living from their goods or service alone. It means that you will stay with them even if the going gets temporarily hard.

Frequently Asked Questions:

Q. *You use the words 'sales agents' but I have never ever heard of the words in the industry I work in?*

A. There are many descriptions such as 'commission only salesperson', 'agent', 'sales consultant' etc., but for simplicity we will describe all the activities described in this book as sales agents.

Q. *It all sounds very easy and the selling side is no different to what I have been doing for employers for some time but what are the pitfalls?*

A.   The pitfalls will be discussed as we get further into the book. The major pitfall at this point is that it must be realised from the outset that a high degree of self-discipline will be called for. You will not have anyone chasing you. You are the boss.

Q.   *What is the worst set back I could have initially?*

A.   Probably the worst thing that can happen to you is that one of your principal's business fails owing you a lot of commission. How to minimise this risk is dealt with later in this book but not relying on one principal alone is the major way to limit the damage.

CASE STUDIES.

Charles Gann, is he in the age trap?.

Charles is a 52 year old sales manager who has just been made redundant for the third time in ten years. He is a good manager of himself and other people and it has not been due to any shortcomings on his part that has caused his redundancy. He is married and his children have grown up and are not a liability. He has a large house but the mortgage is nearly paid. He has some savings that he is prepared to risk.

He has an excellent track record as a sales manager and a salesman and can present himself well. He has made many job applications but has only been offered a couple of interviews that were not successful. He puts the lack of success down to his age, having been sometimes interviewed by much younger people for these jobs. He is becoming rather despondent.

Dennis Wilson is behind in the promotion race.

He is a 30 year old salesman who is dissatisfied with the lack of promotion that he feels is due to him, having had an excellent sales record with both the companies he has worked for since leaving school. He is married and has two young children and a large mortgage. Dennis has a large overdraft.

He feels that his earnings are being limited by his lack of promotion. His present company, like a lot of companies, feels it has to limit the range of salaries earned by its salespeople to avoid disharmony and jealousy. It has long been his ambition to be his own boss but cannot think what to make and sell. He feels that his sales abilities are far greater than those of the people who manage him. This has led to a confrontational attitude in his dealings with his company.

Samantha Grey is getting nowhere in the job-market.

Samantha enjoyed and was extremely successful in a selling job many years ago. She is a 45 year old recently divorced lady who has spent the last 18 years raising a family and building a home. She now wishes to re-enter the business world but has no skills other than her, rather dated, selling skills to offer. After several unsuccessful interviews for a position as a sales representative she thinks her sex and maturity have counted against her. Samantha is a lively, active lady who gets on well with people.

She has her own car and is not short of money. Her need is for a job that will allow her to work the hours she wants, to allow her to follow her hobbies.

Chapter 2

Why the Principal Needs You

YOUR START-UP COST BENEFIT.

The cost to companies of actually employing and putting salespeople on the road is very considerable and variable. Some costs are incurred before the salesperson has even set foot in the door of a customer let alone shown a profit on the orders he gets. If the salesperson is ineffective it may take many months to find this out but salary and costs have to be paid during this time.

The costs of employing salespeople include

- monthly salary
- vehicle costs
- fuel costs
- communication expenses
- national insurance
- hotel costs
- non-productive initial period
- possible sales management costs

Because these costs and the income from sales are variable the company cannot calculate the true cost of a salesperson in its prices. They usually make an educated guess. Always remember, <u>your sales are fixed cost sales</u>. All they have to do is add your fixed commission to their costs.

You are offering.

- no initial costs
- a fixed percentage of commission
- no sales no pay
- no sales management costs

As you are usually working with other principals, you are spreading these costs over, perhaps, several agencies.

Making the principle aware of these benefits.

A considerable number of principals who are offering agencies do not even realise this major benefit or others that we shall mention. They tend to think in the general terms that they cannot afford to employ salespeople and that sales agents are cheaper. If you are fighting hard to gain a wanted agency remember to sell these and other benefits hard to the principal.

Remember, you already have something to sell, your services. It is essential that you know the benefits of your services in order to sell them to a prospective principal.

BRINGING HIM A NEW CUSTOMER BASE.

Most sales agents are ex employed salespeople and choose to work in the industry they have sold in for some time. This sales agent therefore has customers who have been visited for a long time and who buy regularly . Even if the agent does not necessarily already do business with a prospective customer, they know it exists, who is the decision maker and that it is a prospect. This is a major benefit to a principle. You are bringing him an extra, new, potential, customer base immediately. Also as you have probably built up a customer base with your other agencies, you are giving him access to them.

You could bring him

- market knowledge in your chosen area
- access to your existing customer base
- your credibility attached to his offer

Your credibility as a selling point.

It is a fact that 'people buy people', meaning that most buyers, all things being equal, buy from salespeople they like and respect. You as a sales agent will come to know this more than most salespeople. Respect should always be your aim. Most sales agents build up a base of existing customers who buy, or are at least prepared to listen about, further products from the sales agent. They respect the agents judgement.

If you are a new sales agent or are selling into an unknown market area, you do not have this advantage, but at least your principal will not be paying out salaries while a salesperson finds out who the buyers are.

ASSISTING PRODUCT BIASED COMPANIES.

Many companies are what could be described as product biased. This means they are very good at producing the product or service but are not very skilful at selling . The owners probably do not come from a selling background or formed the company in the hope that sales will just appear. Other companies may have spent too much money developing the product or service and do not have enough left over to employ salespeople. As an agent, you have a tremendous amount to offer such companies.

Your advantages.

- you can bring in immediate selling skills
- you can advise on how to present the offer
- there may be flexibility in commission rates

The disadvantages to you.

- the marketing may be non-existent
- you will become an unpaid sales advisor
- establishing these companies may be harder

Identifying the product orientated company.

Your initial questioning, at the time of negotiation, must establish whether you are dealing with this type of company. It is suggested that you avoid this type of company in the initial stages of setting up your agencies as it can be frustrating. Later, once you are established, they can be very lucrative in the long term.

The questions to ask.

- how many sales people have they ever had
- why did they leave
- how do they intend to increase sales
- what is their sales strategy

The answers given to these questions can usually identify a company that is weak in the selling area. You must always satisfy yourself that the product is saleable.

REDUCING YOUR DISADVANTAGES.

You do, of course have disadvantages over an employed salesperson. Your principal has no control over the actual amount of time that you spend promoting his products or services. How much time you spend on each of your agencies is a matter for you alone to decide. Sometimes a retainer is paid by a principal to get you to spend more time on his offer. But this can be a disadvantage discussed later.

A sales agents disadvantages.

- there is no control on time spent on his sales
- he cannot discipline you in any way
- there must be agreement on sales policy
- he must treat you as an independent business

To reduce the significance of these disadvantages you must concentrate your discussions on the benefits of your service.

Retainers, the possible loss of independence.

A string usually attached to a retainer is that the principal will usually insist that you spend a set amount of time on his business. What is more they will wish you to prove that you spend that time on his business. This will mean unproductive paperwork and possible conflict with HMRC over your self-employed status.

A question that must also be addressed is, what happens when you have accepted a retainer and you find you cannot sell the principals product or service? He, being an ordinary human being and thinking his offer is the best on the market, will accuse you of not trying and may try to tarnish your name.

It is however, unusual for principals to offer retainers. When they do there is usually a reason that must be carefully examined. Have they had a succession of agents and failed to hold them and why is an obvious first question?

Allocating your time.

The question of how much time spent on any one agency causes more anxiety with principals than any other aspect of a sales agents daily working life. Every principal ideally would like you to spend all your time selling his product or service.

You must be very careful when discussing the amount of your time spent on a principals behalf and, if needed, diplomatically point out that you have other agencies you have to represent.

However you must spread your selling time fairly amongst your agencies. Nothing is worse to a principal than to pay out commission to a sales agent knowing that he is not spending any time on his behalf. A soon as that principal sees an opportunity to appoint a new agent who <u>will</u> spend time selling on his behalf, the existing agent will lose that agency.

Be fair to principals.

- don't 'collect' agencies
- give each agency some effort
- give up any non-producing agency

WORKING IN TRADITIONAL 'SALES AGENT' INDUSTRIES.

There are many industries where the use of Sales Agents is traditional and has been for many years. Companies that deal direct with retail outlets are probably amongst the largest users of sales agents. The sales agents usually carry a complementary range of products and work to a very tightly scheduled calling pattern on a range of customers, sometimes built up over many years.

Geography also has a bearing on this matter. It is more cost effective to appoint sales agents in the remoter areas of the country, due to the fact that he is covering large areas representing several principals.

It is very easy for people who have experience of calling on retail outlets to make a success of becoming a sales agent in such industries irrespective of whether it is products or services that are offered.

Traditional areas where sales agents operate.

- Scotland
- Northern Ireland
- Wales
- South West England

These are all thinly populated areas with long distances between towns.

traditional industries for sales agents.

- Insurance
- Jewellery
- Finance
- Fashion
- Bookselling
- Retail Selling

FREQUENTLY ASKED QUESTIONS

Q: *I also have to pay myself a salary, pay car expenses etc. How can I make money where it is uneconomic to pay a salesperson?*

A: You have the advantage that you are spreading those same costs over, perhaps, several agencies and you are selling several products or services to each individual buyer. Your expenses also are tax deductible.

Q: *I am thinking of becoming an agent in a market area where I do not know any buyers. Will this be a disadvantage in obtaining agencies?*

A: A principle, whilst he would prefer people experienced in his industry, will usually make a decision in your favour if you can show him you are a good at selling. This includes selling yourself.

Q: *I cannot really see what is wrong with obtaining a retainer. What if several companies offer me a retainer I can put them all together and make a nice living?*

A: It is unusual for principals to offer retainers. When they do there is usually a reason that must be carefully examined. Have they had a succession of agents and failed to hold them and why is an obvious first question?

Case Studies.

Charles sees the way forward

Charles Gann met on old colleague who had become a freelance sales agent some ten years ago. This ex employed salesman had decided to go freelance after several disappointing jobs. He is now driving a up market car, seemed to be earning a good living and said he was very settled in his way of life. He told Charles of his early efforts to establish himself as a freelance sales agent and told him that initially it was the hardest work he had ever experienced but, being his own boss was a great boost to his self-esteem at that time. Now he was established he had principals chasing him to represent them and could afford to be choosy about what agencies he took on.

He gave Charles the names of a couple of companies that he knew were looking for agents and Charles, knowing that he had nothing to lose at this stage, decided to give them a telephone call to find out more about becoming a freelance sales agent.

Dennis is tempted by a retainer.

Dennis Wilson saw an advert in a newspaper for self-employed salespeople that intimated that very high earnings could be obtained by being successful. The company were offering a retainer for the first six months and there was a company car which had to be paid for out of commission earnings. There was a compulsory 14 day training course with all expenses paid. The whole package was subject to Dennis signing an, as yet unseen, agreement on the first day of the training course.

He was running very short of money and as there was not even any interviews for a paid job in prospect he decide to send in a formal application.

Samantha puts out feelers.

Samantha Grey was exploring the possibilities of getting one of her earlier jobs back and spoke to her ex-boss. He told her that they did not now employ salespeople directly but that they had a Sales Agency that did their selling for them. He gave her the name of the person to contact. She also noticed some advertisements in her local paper for what were, in effect, self-employed salespeople.

She decided to go down both avenues and rang the Sales Agency mentioned by her ex-boss and wrote off for details of the jobs offered in the adverts.

Chapter 3

HOW TO SET UP AS A SALES AGENT.

PREPARING A BUSINESS PLAN.

The aim of a business plan and financial forecast is to help you recognises as soon as possible what is involved in starting up as a freelance sales agent, from testing its strength as an idea, to assessing your financial needs.

Always be ruthlessly honest in your estimates. Remember, you will pay the price of any mistakes.

A sales agents financial affairs are relatively simple in business terms. Do not allow anyone to persuade you otherwise.

Your likely expenditure.

The most likely items of <u>initial</u> expenditure are

- Purchase, lease or hire motor vehicle
- petrol and oil
- vehicle service and repairs
- computer and communication costs
- stationary and postage
- office furniture
- rent, heat and light
- accountants costs
- personal insurance and national insurance
- bank charges
- possible loan repayments
- drawings against expected profits

On the matter of drawings, i.e. wages to yourself, remember that they are 'drawings against expected profit' and you will only be taxed on your actual total profit including drawings. Try to take out the lowest drawings you can manage initially.

Other charges, such as accountants costs, will not come in till the second year.

Your likely income.

The likely income from your efforts are extremely difficult to predict with any certainty. Nevertheless you have to make a forecast. All you can do is add up our total predicted expenditure for the year and that will show us the total income we <u>need</u> for the first year without any profit.

This income requirement then can become our total sales forecast for the first year. Do not forget to add the money you are prepared to put in to the business as income, especially if you will be approaching outside finance. They like to see a commitment by you.

FINANCE AND WHERE TO GET IT.

There are many places to get finance but you will find that the relatively small amounts you may need does restrict your choice.

<u>Sources of finance</u>

- your bank
- using a credit card
- finance houses
- possible local Government start up' schemes

You will find a useful guide to government 'start up' loans at https://www.gov.uk/business-finance-support

Try to spread the finance by, for instance, funding the vehicle from a hire purchase company and the balance from any one of these places Try to avoid giving personal guarantees where possible.

DECIDING YOUR WORKING TERRITORY.

The area you work in has a vital bearing on your profitability. If you work over too large a territory you will incur extra travel expenses and rob yourself of selling time. The decided area must however, contain enough potential business and have as many of your existing connections, if any, as possible.

Your decision will also be modified by the areas available for the agencies you will be seeking. Do not make the mistake of covering one geographical area for one principal and a different area for another principal. A slight extension of your area to accommodate a principal will not affect your profitability but major extensions will.

WORKING FROM HOME.

The majority of agents work from home, at least initially. Try to set a room aside to do your paperwork and telephoning. A certain reasonable percentage of heating, lighting and council tax costs can be set against profits. All office equipment is a tax deductible asset.

Essential office equipment.

- Telephone
- Computer
- Printer/Scanner
- Filing Cabinet
- Supply of stationary

As you can see, it does not take much money to start up. To save costs, try buying a second hand filing cabinet

YOUR LEGAL STATUS.

Trading as a 'Sole Trader'

This is the simplest and most used path for Sales Agents.

Forming a limited company.

The decision on whether to form a limited company is best discussed with your accountant. In the early days it is usually more tax efficient to trade as a 'sole trader' or a 'partnership'. You will also find it easier to obtain finance if you are a sole trader. You will have to register the company and file annual returns etc.

Choice of agency name.

You can now give your agency any name you wish, apart from copying another company name, without the need to register with Companies House. You must however put your own name and the company address on all communications.

The choice of company name should be given some thought. Some agents just use their own name or initials and add the word 'marketing' or 'agent' or similar. Try to avoid too grand a title such as 'Worldwide Systems Ltd' as you will raise prospective customers expectations too high. Never try to give the impression of what you are not. Low key credibility seems to work best for sales agents.

MANAGING INCOME TAX AND VAT.

It is essential that you keep proper records in order to prove your income and outgoings to the relevant tax authority. Even if your system consists of two nails on the wall for bills paid and unpaid and sending them to an accountant at your year end, you must keep records. A useful guide for the Self Employed can be found at: https://www.gov.uk/self-employed-records/what-records-to-keep

The income tax position.

Once you have become self-employed you will have to pay tax via the Self-Assessment Scheme. This entails filling in a very complex set of forms that most people pay their accountants to fill in.

You will also have to pay National Insurance Class 2 (Self Employed) contributions monthly and Class 4 contributions based on your profits at the year end. You will have to notify HMRC that you intend to trade. Your Accountant can do this for you and suggest an advantageos starting date. You can find out more at https://www.gov.uk/set-up-sole-trader

HMRC Definition of a Self Employed Person.

There are a strict set of rules surrounding the definition of Self Employment (IR35). The main rules are as follows:

- You must be defined as a 'Worker'
- You must be a 'Sole Trader'
- You must not be an 'Office Holder' for a client
- You must not arrange for someone else to do the work.
- You must not pay someone else to do the work.
- Only you must decide how the work is done.
- Only you must decide the hours to be worked.
- You must agree where you work and not be told.

There is a simple calculator defining 'Self Employment' at: https://www.tax.service.gov.uk/check-employment-status-for-tax/setup.

The V.A.T. position.

Before you start this will need careful consideration. The 'VAT threshold' i.e. the amount of taxable supplies, or commission invoices in your case, before the need to register for V.A.T. has been increasing of late.

You will have to register for VAT.

- if at the end of any month the value of the taxable supplies, i.e. **commission invoices**, you have made in the past twelve months has exceeded the latest threshold figure currently £84,000

- at any time there are reasonable grounds for believing that the value of taxable supplies you will make in the next 30 days will exceed the latest threshold figure currently £84,000

It is therefore unlikely that you will need to register for VAT initially. When you do need to register, there are explanation leaflets available from: https://www.gov.uk/topic/business-tax/vat

USING AN ACCOUNTANT.

The costs of using an accountant ideally should be recouped by the tax he saves you. Respectable accountants usually have good relations and are trusted by local Inland Revenue and can act as a buffer for you in any disagreement on taxation.

They can also act as business advisors and will suggest on matters such as finance, tax efficient pensions and many other financial matters. You will probably be charged for this advice so keep your time with him to the minimum.

Doing your own simple bookkeeping using software packages such as QuickBooks, Zoho, Sage or similar will cut down the cost of using an accountant. They charge by the hour. He is then just checking your figures rather than assembling them. There are many simple computer programmes that can do this easily. Some of these are freeware.

- ask other small businessmen for a recommended accountant.
- make sure he knows what you are trying to achieve
- do your bookkeeping at least quarterly
- keep every business invoice or docket
- submit your figures to him on time.

FREQUENTLY ASKED QUESTIONS

Q. I will find difficulty in estimating my income from commission to put in my budget. How do I do this?

A. Forecasting is an inexact art. All you can do is calculate your expenditure monthly and this becomes your income target. It is how you progress towards this target that matters.

Q. My bank will not advance me any finance without me using my house as a guarantee. How do I get round this problem?

A. Firstly, recalculate your expenditure to see if savings can be made. Then recalculate your expenditure using your credit cards for such items as petrol, stationary etc. thus spreading the credit. You may find you do not need finance.

Q. Can I reclaim the VAT I pay out even if I am not VAT registered?

A. No. Only when you are registered is it possible to reclaim VAT.

CASE STUDIES

Charles Gann did his business plan, budget and cash-flow forecast and finds that, by using some of his redundancy money, he does not really need external finance at least initially. Nevertheless he decides to consult his bank and makes an approach to the small business manager at his local branch. He has never met him and an appointment is made. He has wisely written his cash flow forecast in such a way as to apparently need a small overdraft at one point which he knows he will not really need and can repay at any time. After consideration the bank agrees his overdraft. They have checked his proposal and found it sound.

Dennis Wilson already has a large overdraft. He is certain his bank will not extend it. He completes his business plan and calculates his financial needs. The major expenditure, a car, was to be paid for out of his commission with the company he is in negotiation with. Nevertheless he will need some money while he is starting up. He sees an advert in the local newspaper for cheap loans and contacts the firm. After a few questions over the phone they send him an application form and a few days later offer to lend him what he wants at a slightly high interest rate and over three years.

Samatha Grey calculates that, providing she gets some commission payments in about three months' time she can manage easily without outside finance. Her main problem is that the car that she has is getting old and may need some repairs or even replacement especially with the extra travelling that will be involved with a sales agents life. She decides to wait to see how her estimated budget works out in practice and then purchase a car either through hire purchase or a personal loan from her bank or her building society.

Chapter 4

LOOKING FOR YOUR FIRST AGENCIES.

WHERE TO LOOK FOR SALES AGENCIES.

There are several places to look for agencies. The *AgentBase* newsletter deals exclusively with advertisements from principals looking for agents.. Their address is at the end of this book.

Places to look.

- Online Google Search
- the national daily newspapers
- local newspapers
- AgentBase Newsletter (see Useful Addresses)

While you are looking you will also see many 'get rich quick' schemes that sound like agencies. Do not mistake them for genuine sales agent opportunities.

ASSESSING A GOOD AGENCY.

There are no laid down criteria for a good agency. The worth of an agency will depend on your experience and judgement, however the following points should be addressed.

With a good agency, the product

- can be sold to your existing contacts
- is competitively priced
- is advertised
- does not conflict with another agency
- has a future
- is already selling
- is readily available
- has good descriptive literature

Not every agency will offer every one of these points. If any points are non-existent or weak you must decide, on balance, whether you can find a way round these difficulties without compromising an otherwise good potential agency.

HOW MANY AGENCIES SHOULD YOU HOLD?

There is no hard and fast rule here. New agents will find that two in the first year can be handled within his or her capabilities. With further experience the answer should be, the number of agencies the agent can handle and still give each agency a fair proportion of his time.

There are disturbing number of agents who 'collect' agencies in the hope that they will each bring in some unsolicited business without effort on the sales agents part. Experienced principals, who incidentally tend to offer the best agencies, are aware of such agents and will reject them.

SPECIALISING IN A MARKET SECTOR.

As it is more economic for a sales agent to call on one buyer and sell him several products it is also more efficient to specialise in a market area even if the potential customers are drawn from differing industries.

For instance

- agency 1.   Drinks Vending Machines
- agency 2.   Snack Vending Machines
- agency 3.   Vending supplies

Calling on

- offices
- factories
- warehouses
- canteens
- shops

Market expertise is built up in this way. Most agents chose to operate in a market area that is already known to them. In considering an agency you must ask yourself whether it fits in with your market plan.

APPROACHING A PROEPECTIVE AGENCY

Once you have decided to approach a prospective agency you must contact them to arrange a meeting. This can be done by telephone or in writing or by email. If your initial contact is by telephone you should always confirm the meeting in writing or email. The initial contact must always contain enough information to make the principal interested in you but not too much that will allow him to reject you without seeing you.

An initial contact should

- state where you saw his advertisement
- express your interest
- state your reason for interest
- briefly why you qualify
- hold yourself ready for a meeting

PRODUCING AN AGENCY PROFILE.

This is in reality a 'business C.V.' and is best used at a first meeting with a prospective principal. It must give a professional image and be neatly presented. You are trying to establish your credentials as an independent business person. Previous C.V.s were probably trying to establish yourself as a good employee.

A typical agency profile might contain:

Header page

- the words 'AN AGENCY PROFILE'
- the proposed name of your company
- your business address

page 1.

- your bank address
- your accountants address
- your solicitors address
- if applicable, your formation date

page 2.

- the aims of your agency
- your qualifications to hold the agency
- any other agencies held
- third party references

page 3

- a list of typical customers

If you are new to being a sales agent do not hide the fact but stress your previous customers even if they are not relevant to the prospective agency. The document should be well spaced and neat and preferably bound. The use of Microsoft Word, PowerPoint or free Word Processor will help here.

FREQUENTLY ASKED QUESTIONS

Q. *How do I tell genuine agency opportunities from 'get rich quick' schemes?*

A. Generally speaking the 'get rich quick' schemes ask you to pay money in order to gain the agency. Apart from franchises, be wary of any initial monetary involvement.

Q. *Why is an exclusive area important?*

A. Exclusivity means you will get paid a commission on that area however the order originates. For example, should your customer telephone his order in, you will still get the commission. Agencies that only pay you commission on the orders you physically get are to be avoided at all costs.

Q.   *I am employed as a salesmen in an industry that is running down. Should I move into a new industry?*

A.   Remember that you will have a learning period if you move. It is probably better to take one agency in your old business in order to retain some income and develop a long term strategy to change industries

CASE STUDIES.

Charles Gann was following up the couple of prospective agencies that his ex-colleague had mentioned. He telephoned the sales manager of one and made an appointment for the following week. He could not contact the relevant person of the other company so he decided to write. The letter was brief, to the point and did not say much more than he understood they were looking for an agent and that he would be interested in discussing this with them. He invited them to telephone him.

Dennis Wilson contacted the company and found that they were offering the retainer for sales agents together with the loan for car purchases. They sent him details which included expensively printed testimonials from sales people stating how working for the company, which made cosmetics and sold them direct to the consumer, had changed their lives. The company booked him on to the next training course and said they would discuss further details with him during this course.

Samantha Grey spoke to the sales manager of the sales agency that was acting on behalf of her previous company. He said that there was a vacancy on the territory that she was interested in and invited her to an interview in about a months' time. She also followed up on the advertisements she had seen and sent them all a letter and C.V. All the agencies were in different fields but, at this stage she did not think this would cause a problem.

Chapter 5

SELLING YOURSELF TO THE PRINCIPAL.

CHOOSING THE VENUE.

At least one meeting to discuss the agency is inevitable. Try to arrange to visit the principal at his place of work rather than on neutral or your own territory. The reason for this is that there are many subtle signs that can be read if you visit him.

- are his works or offices run-down?
- does the telephone ring much while you are there?
- is there a calm business-like atmosphere?
- how does he relate to his staff?
- does the company appear well-established?

The answers to questions such as these can help you make the decision on whether to take the agency.

If you do meet away from his works or offices try to ensure that you can visit them before you finally agree anything.

WHAT THE PRINCIPAL WILL BE LOOKING FOR.

The principal will be firstly looking for a good salesperson and secondly for a well-connected agent. If this is an attempt to get your first agency, try to get some third-party references to your selling abilities to take to the meeting. Failing this, take a list of the type of customers you already deal with. Do not, of course, leave this list with him.

His first priority is to take on a salesperson that he thinks will be successful for his product or service. You are being interviewed as a salesman rather than an agent at this stage. Before any other matter is discussed you must impress him as a salesperson. The more evidence of this that you can produce the better.

WHAT YOU SHOULD BE LOOKING FOR.

At a first meeting you should be looking for:

- a competitive product or service
- a reasonable commission
- an agreed, exclusive territory
- acceptable literature & marketing
- sales aids
- advertising and lead generation
- a degree of training if necessary
- a formal, written agreement

These are all basic needs and your own experience will tell you what is acceptable. The formal agreement is dealt with in greater detail in chapter 7.

Other points you must agree.

- how and when you will get paid
- what happens with bad debts
- what paperwork do they want
- will they pre-notify any 'house accounts'
- your limits on price negotiation
- who deals with after-sales service

Getting paid.

The most important point here is about getting paid. <u>Never</u> accept a situation where you get your commission only when the customer has paid. You will usually wait a long time.

Bad debts.

It is quite usual for a principal to deduct commission from commission owing due to a bad debt. You must jointly agree on the period that will elapse before it is deemed a bad debt.

Paperwork.

Paperwork is another potential difficulty. Time spent on paperwork is non-earning time for a sales agent. It is generally accepted that a principal is entitled to a monthly report of your activities on his behalf and any observations on such matters as market trends and competitors activities. He needs this information to help you in the market. Submitting daily or weekly reports should be diplomatically resisted at all costs.

House accounts.

Another area of potential problems are 'house accounts' where the principal has dealt with a customer for a long time and claims that <u>he</u> has gained the business and need not pay a commission on it. It is vital that he declares who these are at the outset. There is nothing worse for an agent than getting orders from a customer only to have the principal claim it as a 'house account' and not pay commission. Another point arises on servicing the 'house accounts'. It is unfair to ask an agent to service these accounts without payment.

Negotiation limits.

Agreeing the limits of the agents authority in dealing with prices or any other promises made on behalf of the principal is another point that must be agreed. The sales agent must know how far he can go in negotiations without reference to the principal.

After-sales servicing.

After-sales servicing can be expensive in areas such as machinery sales and many other fields. If it is likely to crop up, agree who is to carry this out and at whose cost before signing the agreement.

ASKING THE RIGHT QUESTIONS.

You will find that a check list of all the above will enable you to ask the right questions. There is nothing worse than leaving an interview and thinking of unasked questions on important matters.

You will find that asking these questions will enhance your credibility with the prospective principal. He will recognise that, even if you are a new sales agent, you know what is involved in running a sales agents business.

One of the questions is, of course, about what happened to your predecessor. A lot can be revealed about the principals attitude to agents by the answer to that question.

MANAGING THE INTERVIEW.

Due to the unique relationship you will be entering into with the principal, the interview will be rather different to a job interview. You are a potential investor in his business. You are going to invest your time and money in promoting his product or service. You must get this point across at all costs.

The interview will be more balanced than the usual job interview with you wanting to know far more than you would if you were looking for employment. You will, in effect, be interviewing him.

It would not be wise to commit yourself at the first or only interview. There are issues, such as the written agreement, that must be studied before making a final decision. If the principal has not given you a copy of his proposed agreement, ask for a copy to be communicated to you and tell him you will give him a decision after you have studied it.

MANAGING THE FOLLOW-UP.

After your meeting it is considered polite to communicate with the principal and thank him for his courtesy and interest. In this communication you should briefly outline any agreements that were jointly reached that you do not expect to be part of the written agreement.

The possibility of extending your area after a trial period is the sort of verbal agreement that probably will not be in the formal agreement.

All this will re-enforce your professionalism.

FREQUENTLY ASKED QUESTIONS

Q. The principal I am negotiating with is adamant that he will not pay my commission until he gets paid. He is new in the business and says he cannot afford to take the chance of paying commission and not getting paid himself. What do I do?

A. Explain that you have no objection to repaying the commission should the customer default. Should his fears be based on cash flow problems perhaps you can negotiate an initial period of 'commission on customer payment' and then change to a more normal arrangement. By that time you may have become invaluable to him and you will be in a better negotiating position.

Q. The principal wants weekly reports of my activities on his behalf and reports on my actions on any sales leads he supplies. Shall I agree?

A It depends on your assessment of the worth of the agency. You are likely to spend a lot of either your spare time or your selling time servicing his paperwork needs. It is not unusual for principals to request reports on genuine sales leads they supply. They have spent money obtaining them and they wish to judge the effectiveness of them.

Q. The principal claims he has some house accounts on the area we are discussing but is avoiding naming them, he says, for commercial reasons. Shall I continue negotiating?

A. Successful agencies are based on mutual trust. Make it a condition of your agreement that he names these accounts should he offer you an agreement. If he refuses you will never be able to have complete trust in him.

CASE STUDIES.

CHARLES GANN received a telephone call from the Managing Director of S.Y Systems, the company he had written to. He invited Charles to a meeting the following week at his offices. This meant he now had two appointments to discuss agencies. At the meeting with S.Y Systems he was most impressed with the way the company seemed to be run and he was shown the products. He was sure he could sell them to his old customers.

Charles showed the M.D. the company profile he had prepared. They went through it together and the M.D. remarked that he noticed that Charles had not got any agency experience. Charles countered by saying that though he was not an experienced agent he had all the right attributes, namely, sales experience, a customer base and enough money to tide him over until he was established. He told the M.D. that he intended to take on other, non-competing, agencies.

The M.D. accepted this and said that, at this stage, he was quite prepared to offer Charles the agency in writing. Charles asked that a copy of the written agreement be sent to him for his comment. This was agreed.

Dennis Wilson attended the training course at a nearby hotel but found he was not really required to sell himself to the principal. In fact the major problem was to identify who was in charge. The days were taken up by very professional presentations and videos by various members of the company's executives. At no time did anyone discuss his sales experience or personal circumstances.

He found out that he was expected to pay for his samples and literature. He also found that his commission rate was weighted in such a way that he had to find other salespeople to earn maximum commission. The company offered to lend him the money for his samples together with the loan for the car and deduct it from his future commission.

The training course ran late and ended in a hurry with no chance for Dennis to talk to anyone about the agreement. He was told that the folder he had been given contained two copies of the agreement and would he sign it and return one copy to the company?

Samantha Grey attended the interview offered to her by the sales agency. She was rather shocked to find that the offices were rather dirty, the Sales Director was late for the appointment and, during the appointment the telephone rang many times. He apologised and left the room to answer the calls each time. He seemed flustered each time he returned.

Without even reading Samantha's expensively produced company profile he offered Samantha the agency. The commission rates seemed extremely good and far better than she had expected. She was told that new literature was being prepared and that they had run out of the existing literature so she could not take any away to look at.

The written agreement would be put in the post to her and a start date was mentioned but Samantha, wisely, said she wanted time

Chapter 6

NEGOTIATING THE FORMAL AGREEMENT.

REQUESTING AN AGREEMENT.

A written agreement should be considered an absolute necessity with any agency. When it is jointly signed it should be put away for safekeeping and hopefully never consulted again. It is a sign that something has gone wrong with your relationship if you are viewing your agreement regularly.

Some agents have held agencies for many years based on little more than a handshake and goodwill. In today's business world this is a risky situation. Early in your negotiations ask for a written agreement and view any reluctance to provide this with suspicion. If the Principal does not have a standard agency agreement get him to contact AgentBase who can sell him a model agreement that has been drawn up by a Solicitor that is familiar with Sales Agents practice and the laws governing the same.

REGULATIONS ON COMMERCIAL AGENTS AGREEMENTS.

There is in existence a European Council directive on agency agreements, *The Commercial Agents Regulations (1993)*, that standardises some parts of such agreements across the whole of the E.U. It also gives the force of law to these clauses <u>whether there is a written agreement or not.</u> An outline of the Regulations are laid out in appendix 1.

This is the first recognition of the legal status of a commercial agent in U.K. civil law. In the past, the standing of the written agreement was based on the law of contract. This law has many interpretations and does not specifically deal with agents. Nevertheless, the E.C. directive contains many clauses such as 'reasonable' and 'good faith' which have yet to be tested in the U.K. Courts.

Many principals with existing agreements have tried and are trying to find ways round this legislation mainly due to its compensation or indemnity owing to the agent on the ending of the agency. One way is to actually employ the agent but only pay him a commission on sales. This, of course, destroys the self-employed status of the agent with its advantages to both parties.

As a new agent you should not come across this problem.

THE ELEMENTS OF THE AGREEMENT.

The written agreement should deal with the following points.

* the geographical area or type of customer.
* exclusivity of area of operation
* commission rates and when payable
* the products
* termination of the agreement
* supply of sales aids
* the negotiation limits
* what house accounts are there
* paperwork requirements
* notification of orders placed direct

The negotiable clauses.

All these points are negotiable of course. Some principals who have an existing team of agents, may not wish to vary their existing agreement. Although specific mention of the E.C. directive may not neccassarily be made in the agreement, the directive states that the regulations shall apply to all agreements made after 1st January 1994.

IF THE AGREEMENT IS BREACHED.

All agreements, in reality, rely mainly on trust and goodwill between two parties. The alternative is costly legal argument. There are as many unwritten rules in the relationship as there are clauses in the written agreement. Try to foster an open and honest attitude to your principal.

The first rule, if a breach of agreement becomes obvious to either party, is not to go to law immediately. If you think the agreement has been breached by the principal meet him to discuss it. In many cases it will be a pure oversight on his part and he will rectify it and apologise.

If the breach seems deliberate, again meet him to voice your point of view and then confirm your points in writing. Should he not be moved into rectifying the situation you then have a decision to make. Do you resort to the law or do you carry out the ultimate sanction and withdraw from the agreement and take your customers with you?

Each individual case will vary and this is a decision that you alone can take. It must be borne in mind that your relationship has broken down and that no amount of legal procedures will put it together again. If it is a monetary matter the amount you could lose through legal action should be taken into account.

FREQUENTLY ASKED QUESTIONS

Q. The principal says he knows nothing of the E.C. Directive on Agents Agreements and wants nothing to do with it. Do I go on negotiating?

A. Do let him know that the clauses in the directive have the force of law and override any similar clauses in any written agreement. The clauses also have the force of law whether there is a written agreement or not. The directive does not contain any measures that could not be expected in an agreement between to equal and honourable parties.

Q. There are other agents working for the principal on the area we are talking about. Should I sign the agreement?

A. Do not sign the agreement until you have established an area as exclusive to you. Whether this area is geographical or market based is up to the individual circumstances. You could find the results of your efforts going to someone else's pocket including the principals.

Q. The sales aids provided are very expensive and the principal wants me to pay for them. Do I buy them?

A. As a general rule no. Offer to give him a deposit on them if he is insistent. The question arises as to what happens when the sales aids need renewing or a new model or service is launched.

CASE STUDIES.

Charles Gann received the formal agreement in the post a couple of days later. He checked it against what was said at the meeting. He also checked it against the E.C. directive on agency agreements and noticed that there were no references to either compensation or indemnity should they decide to dispense with his services at some time in the future.

He also noticed that the time scale of the notice period was one month for both parties throughout the life of the agreement. This did not match the E.C. directive that had a sliding scale dictating up to a maximum three months' notice after the commencement of the third year of the agreement.

Charles rang the principal who apologised and said that they did know there was an E.C. Directive but did not know what was in it. They said they would match anything in the directive and promised to consult their solicitor and send him a new agreement.

Dennis Wilson read the agreement he was given on the training course. He noticed that there was no exclusivity on the area and that the company reserved the right to appoint other agents on his area at their own discretion. He also noticed that, even though the loan for the car and samples were mentioned, no interest rate was specified. He wished he had clarified this point on the training course but he remembered they had not given him time.

He contacted them but had difficulty in finding the right person. When he eventually spoke to the Sales Manager, who he had not met, he said that they would not take on any other sales agent for his area and that clause in the agreement was a safety measure on the companies part.

Regarding the interest on the loan for the car and samples, this would be at a floating rate. Dennis had to break off the conversation because his new car had just arrived.

Samantha Grey waited a couple of weeks and, having not received the promised agreement, telephoned the Sales Director. He said that they had given the matter some thought and that, due to a report from their solicitor on the effect of the E.C. directive, they were postponing sending the agreement to her. They still wanted her to start as an agent. She said she would not start without a formal agreement being signed.

Samantha was getting worried about the time it was taking and decided to chase up some of the other agencies she had written after. A couple of telephone calls soon established that both the companies were still actively looking for agents and had not contacted her for, what seemed, perfectly valid reasons.

Chapter 7

CARRYING OUT CHECKS ON THE PRINCIPAL.

CHECKING WITH YOUR BANK.

It is obvious that if you take on an agency with an unsound principal your investment in time, travel and incidental expenses will be at risk. All steps should be taken to ensure that you are acting for a company that can and will deliver the goods or service and pay your commission on time.

This is one of the easiest checks to make but it will tell you little apart from his banks assessment of his creditworthiness at the time of asking. You will need to tell your bank his banks address and his correct trading title. Ask him for this information during your first interview. It should demonstrate to him your caution in money matters. You will also have to let your bank know how much you think he will owe you at any one time. This will have to be a guess on your part.

The answer from your bank will be couched in bankers terms and will probably say something like ' ABCD is good for the amount stated'. This does not tell you a lot as his bank would hardly advertise the fact that they think his business is risky and thereby affect his trading.

USING A CREDIT INFORMATION AGENCY.

There are many credit investigation companies who will give you a far more independent assessment of the company you are intending to take an agency with. Their assessment is based on other companies actual trading experience. Many credit investigation companies are listed online. You will have to pay for these services.

COMPANIES HOUSE WEBSITE

A lot of information can be gleaned from the Companies House Website: https://beta.companieshouse.gov.uk Make sure you have the correct name for the company you are searching on.

IDENTIFYING A RISKY PRINCIPAL.

This is a most difficult thing to do. Apart from the credit checks mentioned and if you are staying in the industry you previously sold in, ask your customers about your prospective principal. It is amazing how risky companies draw attention to themselves.

possible signs of a risky principal

- late deliveries
- undue debt chasing
- regular and large discounting
- recent name changes
- stock shortages
- high staff turnover
- extravagant product claims
- will not name satisfied customer

The main aim is to keep your eyes and ears open. Constantly watch for the signs and be prepared to act on them.

SPEAK TO HIS EXISTING AGENTS.

At the interview ask him for the name and telephone number of a couple of his existing sales agents and telephone them. Usually they will give you an honest assessment of the principal from the agents point of view. They are not employed by him so they have no need to give a dishonest answer.

FREQUENTLY ASKED QUESTIONS

Q. Being already in the same business as my prospective agency I asked one of my customers about the principal and he was most uncomplimentary. Shall I pull out of negotiations?

A. Make further investigations and if you receive similar answers from other customers go carefully. Do not take the first customers views in isolation. The problem may have been caused by the customer.

Q. It is obvious that the principal has had a high turnover of agents recently. How can I find out the reason?

A. Some detective work is called for. Through a third party, try to find the name and telephone number of one of his agents, either past or present, and contact the agent. You must take whatever is said on its face value and use it as background knowledge.

Q. I do not believe the claims that the principal is making about his product. How do I check?

A. Take a guess on who his customers should be and telephone them and ask them politely what they think of the product or service? Bad news travels fast and they will soon tell you if the product or service is not as good as is claimed

CASE STUDIES.

Charles Gann was waiting for the new written agreement to arrive and used this time to do some credit checks on the principal. He wrote to his bank quoting the bank details he had been given and told them how much he expected to be invoicing them monthly. He received a reply some ten days later that said that they were ' a well-run company who would not enter into debts they could not service'.

Charles thought that this was a bit vague and decided to contact a credit checking agency that he found in the Yellow Pages Directory. He telephoned them and they told him that if he wrote, enclosed all the details and a cheque for twenty pounds, they would give him a credit rating for the company. He did this and received a reply by return of post that was a complete breakdown of the company's financial affairs going back some five years and a credit rating that far exceeded the figure that he had in mind.

He felt completely happy with the financial stability of the company. He also received the new written agreement, checked it and could not find any major problems.

He telephoned the principal and told him he was going to sign the agreement and they arranged a starting date.

Dennis Wilson was having one of his regular meetings with his bank manager about his overdraft. He updated the manager with his negotiations so far. The bank manager suggested that he ought to make a credit check on the company and offered to do it on his behalf if he could send him the details. Dennis agreed. He tried various persons within the company but could not get anyone to give him the details he wanted.

The sales director of the company telephoned to say that he wanted Dennis to start selling on their behalf next week. Dennis told him that he still was not satisfied with the agreement as it stood but the sales director said they could sort the matter out afterwards.

Dennis decided to go ahead and start as he was desperately short of money.

Samantha Grey received a letter from the company saying that they could not change the agreement to fall in line with the E.C..Directive but they would like her to start selling for them using their standard agreement. Samantha did not commit herself and gave them some excuses why she could not sign and start selling for them yet.

She had interviews with the other two companies and they both came up to the criteria she had set. They both meant calling on the same customers, the commissions were adequate and the written agreements, although slightly different, were to her satisfaction.

She accepted both the agencies and wrote a polite letter to the first agency declining their offer. She arranged a starting date for both.

Chapter 8

RUNNING YOUR AGENCY.

BUYING AND RUNNING A CAR.

This is an area of your operation that needs great thought. A vehicle that constantly lets you down can affect your earnings. For example lateness or cancellation of appointments can affect your credibility with your customers. On the other hand an expensive, up-market car with its high running costs could sink your agency in its initial stages. It is better to wait till you can afford the expensive car you always wanted.

Many agents run, and can afford to run, far more expensive cars than their employed counterparts but they usually wait until they can afford it. Even if you are used to having the latest model of an executive saloon, supplied by your employer of course, do not be afraid of being seen in a clean, well maintained second hand car.

.Do make sure that your insure covers business use and tell your insurer that it will be used for 'Commercial Travelling' Nowadays there is not usually an extra charge for this.

Ways of financing a vehicle.

There are many ways of financing the purchase of a car and your choice will be dictated by your circumstances. In the initial stages it is wiser to try to avoid long term and heavy financial commitments. Vehicles can be financed by

- Buying a car using a personal loan.

- Hire purchase (HP) to finance a new car.

- Personal contract purchase (PCP)

- Leasing - Personal contract hire (PCH)

- Using a credit card to buy a car…

If you are being made redundant by your company it may be possible to arrange to take over the car you are driving at present always assuming it is in good condition.

INVOICING AND CHASING YOUR COMMISSION.

One of the most important and satisfying aspects of your agency is invoicing your commission. Some of your principals may be in a 'self-billing scheme' for VAT purposes and you may not need to invoice them, but the majority will need an invoice from you. These invoices can be simply typed out on your own letter-headed notepaper.

Always keep a record of orders placed through yourself. Your written agreement should have provided that the principal notifies you of all orders that are placed direct with him on your area and are commissionable. This normally means a monthly statement from him that you check and invoice accordingly.

When the commission is due is dependent on your agreement with the principal. A usual arrangement is at the month end following the month of invoice.

Chasing your commission.

Never fail to chase any late payment of a commission invoice. politely point out to your principal that your invoices are both wages and expenses to you. Should he pay the wages and expenses of his employees late he would soon find himself looking for new employees. You are no exception.

MANAGING YOUR FINANCES.

We have already dealt with budgeting and cash-flow forecasting in an earlier chapter. It is vital that you monitor your progress towards these targets on a regular basis. Do not make this an obsession but do spend a half hour or so a month checking your progress. If you are running into financial problems, the earlier you spot it the earlier you can take remedial action.

Paying your bills is another matter that has to be attended to regularly. Try to arrange a set time in the month to receive your bank statement and, <u>at that time</u>, sit down and plan what bills you have to pay and what income you will have to pay them.

A simple idea is to have two files, one for bills yet to be paid and one for those already paid. Monthly action on the bills 'yet to be paid file' will keep you in your suppliers good books. If you find your cash-flow will not allow you to pay some bills, pay part of them and contact the suppliers and give them an estimate of when you can pay the balance <u>and stick to that estimate</u>. Do not ignore bills you cannot pay.

Another way of spreading the finances is to pay as much as possible by credit card. This means that, should you be in a lean period you can pay the minimum amount and then completely clear your debt when you have a good month. Beware building up a large debt on your credit cards due to the relatively high interest rates.

COMMUNICATION WITH YOUR PRINCIPALS.

It is vital that you keep in touch with your principals on a regular basis. They wish to know what is going on in your area. There is nothing worse to a principal than not to hear from an agent for weeks or even months. He automatically thinks you are not promoting his product. You may be working extremely hard on his behalf but lack of contact can, quite mistakenly, lead to him thinking the worse.

You must always, as a matter of courtesy and efficiency, let all your principals know if you are going on holiday, are off work sick or are absent for any other reason.

Even if you are failing to get orders for him, contact him and discuss ways that you can jointly increase the business.

Submitting monthly reports.

Any business-like principal will ask you for a monthly report of the activity on your area. It is sometimes a bit irksome but do remember he has to plan his production or stock levels or finances on market information. Your estimate of market trends, orders in the pipeline and your business in negotiation, together with the estimates from his other agents can give him the information he needs to help you.

You may be disinclined to go into too much detail regarding your contacts, but a general outline should suffice. It is usually sufficient to say that you are expecting an order worth ,500 from XYZ Ltd rather than you are dealing with Fred Bloggs of XYZ Ltd.

It is wise to resist any attempt by the principle to get you to report on a daily or weekly basis. However reports on special projects he may initiate are quite in order. He is trying to help you, you must try to help him.

THE IMPORTANCE OF JOURNEY PLANNING.

This is a phrase that often crops up with regard to paid salespeople and is often given little attention. Now that you will be paying the travelling expenses it does become extremely important. It is beyond the scope of this book to discuss journey planning, any good salesperson will know the basics. Trying to keep to an efficient journey plan has a two-fold benefit to you. It maximises your selling time and decreases your expenses.

Making appointments.

The importance of making appointments for every call depends on the industry you work in. In retail selling it is less important than being expected a certain time of the month for your regular customers and making appointments to see new prospects. In selling capital goods such as machinery etc., appointments are vital.

Try and set a fixed time every week to telephone for appointments with new prospects. The knowledge that the person you wish to speak to is actually there when you call is a financial consideration for an agent.

PROTECTING YOUR LEGAL RIGHTS.

There is an organisation called the Professional Sales Association, (PSA), that is part of the UNITE Union. Its primary existence is to guide you and protect your legal rights as a Sales Agent. It holds regular Seminars on Legal matters in various parts of the country. It also offers free legal advice via Solicitors who are well versed in Sales Agents activities. As well as advice it can even pay legal fees for taking winnable cases to court. It even paid to take a case up to the House of Lords in Lonsdale vs Howard and Hallam Ltd. Most cases are about compensation or indemnity. And large sums have been won on behalf of wronged Sales Agents. There are other benefits too. At about £3.35 a week it is excellent insurance. They can be found at: https://unitetheunion.org/psa

FREQUENTLY ASKED QUESTIONS

Q. The principal says he cannot send me a statement of commission earned every month and that I will have to claim the commission earned. What is the danger in this?

A. The danger here is that you have no record of any orders that your customer has placed direct with him. If he were dishonourable he could pocket the commission on these orders without you knowing. For a time!

Q. How often should I communicate with a principal?

A. There is no hard a fast rule here. In an active business relationship once a week is not too often. Once a month would tend to put a strain on the relationship.

CASE STUDIES.

Charles Gann started looking for a car. He decided he would go for a low-mileage, second hand executive model. He thought they represented excellent value for money as the, so called, 'write down', meaning the drop in value from new to second hand, on this type of vehicle is high. He visited a vehicle leasing company who were selling some of their ex-lease cars and found an excellent car some three years old with high mileage but well maintained.

He arranged hire purchase through the leasing company. He could have purchased the car outright but felt he would like to retain as much financial reserve as he could. If things went well he could always pay the hire purchase off early and save interest payment. He made sure that there were minimum early payment penalties in the H.P. agreement.

Dennis Wilson was already equipped with a new car, to be paid for by deductions from his commissions. He was now ready to go out selling. He was keen to get earning because his bank were chasing him hard to reduce his overdraft.

Dennis started telephoning potential customers and found that he was very coldly received and, after having spent a couple of days on the telephone, he found he had only managed to obtain two appointments. He was a bit annoyed by a telephone call from his principal at the end of his first week asking him for a breakdown of his appointments for the following week. There was a form to fill in and, even though he was slightly uneasy about it, he filled it in.

Over the next few weeks Dennis found himself spending most of his time on the telephone trying to get appointments. He did get some but the ratio was about ten phone calls to one appointment. When on the appointments with the prospective customers he found that they found every excuse not to buy the product.

Dennis started to realise that he had made a bad choice of either principal or product but he was committed to paying for his car and samples.

Samantha Grey was using the car that she already owned so that was one decision she did not have to make. She decided that she would buy a computer, mainly for its word processing capability. She was not very good at typing and wanted to do lots of mail-shots herself to save the costs of using a secretarial bureau.

She had budgeted for this item together with the other things she needed such as an office desk, a telephone answering machine and all the other items that are found in an efficient and modern office.

It was while she was connecting the computer up that she received a telephone call from one of her new principals telling her that an interested potential customer had telephoned them asking to see someone about their offer. Could she telephone the customer and take the appointment? Samantha was on the way to making her first commission cheque.

CHAPTER 9

SALES AGENTS AND THE DIGITAL AGE.

HOW TECHNOLOGY HELPS YOUR BUSINESS

In general terms digital technology has had a positive impact on the lives of sales agents, with the use of sophisticated software, App's and cloud based programs a Sales Agents life has become far easier and cost effective.

- Search platforms such as Google and Bing have made bus life easier. Gone are the days of thumbing through the Yellow Pages or using directory enquires to find contact details for prospects.

- On-line Data programs and APP's via the Cloud, Customer Relationship Managers, (CRM's), Accounts packages and even virtual offices, help us manage our businesses far more efficiently and the good news is many of these are either low cost or in some cases free.

- Software packages such as presentation programs including the use of images and video help to increase our credibility and professional image. Sophisticated word processing, Email linked to electronic diaries and spreadsheet data analysis all contribute to business efficiency.

- Communication via email, video conferencing such as; Skype, Facetime and many others, help efficiency by reducing the frequency of customer visits and ultimately reducing costs.

HOW TO DEAL WITH PRINCIPALS WHO USE DIRECT SELLING WEBSITES

However, on the negative side of the technology boom, many companies have developed direct sales via Websites and either dispensed with Salespeople or reduced their numbers. An important question must be asked at the interview stage is, does the Principal sell direct via a website and, if so, how is commission to be paid on such sales? A fair way of doing this is to pay the Sales Agent a smaller commission on such sales pointing out to the principal that he, the Salesman, will be in competition with the Principal with regard to selling the Principals product but he has certain advantages. The Sales Agent can offer the principles and customers skills that are difficult for digital platforms to replicate such as:

- Interpersonal skills; the old adage "people buy from people" is still relevant today, as buying either a new product or service is often an emotional event that requires human interaction.

- Customer service; customers will often require salespeople to problem solve for them and deliver a solution in the form of a product or service; this will involve a degree of caring and helping by the salesperson, which again are human traits valued by customers.

- Trust; customers also need to trust their supplier will supply the product or service on offer, again trust is a very strong emotion that can only be strengthened by human interaction with the salesperson.

The use of technology to communicate is changing the way we interact in business and perhaps this book can only highlight a small section of this huge subject by discussing how sales agents and their principles can benefit from it.

We have come a long way since the era of landline telephones and fax machines in the 1980's, not only has our society become increasingly mobile, but so has our communication, with the introduction of smartphones and a wide choice of operating systems including Google Android and Apple iOS we can communicate with our customers just about anywhere in the UK and even worldwide.

USING SOCIAL MEDIA.

With the huge growth in social media the possibilities for sales are endless and can help to drive sales for an agent but in some market sectors the benefits are limited, but in others it can be substantial.

The use of Facebook, Twitter, LinkedIn and many others all come under the heading of *Social Selling* and one of the key ways to do this is via open discussion on Social media, this involves B2B networking online and reaching out to new prospects, educating them in how your product and service can help them and then nurture that connection through interesting content.

It's a new and exciting business world that is being embraced by salespeople all over the UK and delivering sales success at a relatively low cost, so it is recommended that sales agents invest some time in researching how the use of technology can help your business.

Chapter 10

DEVELOPING YOUR CUSTOMER BASE.

THE AGENTS INDEPENDENT ROLE.

As an agent you must do all you can to stress your independence. Most buyers in the UK are used to being called on mainly by employed salespeople and, if not told otherwise, will treat you in the same light. They expect employed salespeople to give them a biased view. They make their assessments on this view.

Find every opportunity to reinforce your role as an advisor rather than a salesperson. A useful tactic is to tell him of your other agencies, even if they are of no interest to him as a buyer. Always say 'they' rather than 'we' when talking to him about any of the agencies you hold. Always be ready to take the customers side, assuming he is correct, in any dispute with your principal. Remember they are your customers! They are your main asset.

It is quite usual to find agents that hold their customers in greater regard than their principals. As with many things it is a matter of balance.

KEEPING YOUR CUSTOMERS INFORMED.

This is an important feature of your life as a sales agent. Do not leave it to each principal to decide whether to inform your customers of the latest developments in his range. If necessary prompt him. An agent should possibly do this himself, if only to reinforce his role as an advisor.

Some ways of informing customers:

- calling on them
- telephoning them..
- mail-shots from principals
- email-shots from the agent

Mail-shots from a principal.

Many principals will have the ability to send their own mail-shots to both your customers and any lists of prospective customers they may purchase. Try to make sure that he co-ordinates these mail-shots with your efforts. It can be very frustrating to be diverted from a planned activity to deal with the inevitable enquiries these bring.

You may be asked for advice on the context and wording of the mail-shot. The following points on mail-shots from you should be borne in mind.

Mail-shots from the agent.

This is an excellent way of getting new information across to all your customers quickly and far more cheaply than calling on them all. They can be achieved by using a suitable word processor with a mail-merge facility on a computer, or by giving your mail-shot letter and a list of customers to a bureau. The latter will, of course, be more costly.

It is important that, with existing customers, you address the greeting in the letter to the customer in the form you usually use to greet him. It is a bit absurd to address the letter 'Dear Sir' when you have greeted the customer as 'Fred' for the past ten years. By all means address prospective customers as 'Dear Sir', it is respectful to do so.

Above all, your mail-shot should inform and invite some form of action from the customer such as 'telephone me on 01545 778990' or 'speak to Julie Wright'.

PROMOTING YOUR FULL RANGE.

The advantage you have over employed salespeople is that you have more than one product or product range to sell. This advantage increases where you can sell more than one product to an individual customer. This initially calls for a lot of trust on your customers part but, providing you have chosen your agencies carefully and when he is happy with the second product sold him, he will come to rely on you for even more products you may offer.

This is when an agent really comes into his own. Use every opportunity to show him new products, even consult him on any new agency you are thinking of taking on. Do not betray this trust by selling him something you are not fully satisfied with. It takes a long time to build up this trust but only one bad sale to ruin it.

HELPING YOUR PRINCIPAL GET PAID.

Some customers run into cash-flow problems from time to time. It is a good tactic to get your principal to contact you whenever he is worried about a payment from your customer, before he sends a threatening legal letter. You can then approach the customer in a quiet and appropriate manner. Explaining to the customer that you will not get paid if he defaults will usually bring results, but not necessarily quick results.

Dealing with disputed invoices.

It is in your best interests to see that your principal gets paid. Make sure that, if the money is in dispute, that you help both parties to resolve the dispute. This may take some time and effort but it is partly your money they are in dispute over.

Handling complaints.

This is a very important and sensitive area for a sales agent. He must do all he can to resolve the complaint from an individual standpoint and remember that, even if the complaint is unjustified, the customer thinks it is justified. The agent must take the matter up with the principal promptly and monitor the results. Promptly dealing with complaints is one way of preventing them snowballing.

Not over committing principals.

It is a wise rule never to commit a principal to an action without you contact him first.

Typical unauthorised promises

- special samples
- fast deliveries
- product changes
- service visits
- special prices
- longer credit terms

Should the agent be foolish enough to make unauthorised promises on behalf of the principal in such areas and the principal does, or cannot, agree, the agent's credibility suffers with both parties. From the customers viewpoint the agent made the promise which the agent cannot keep. From the principals point of view the agent has made a promise which the principal cannot keep.

FREQUENTLY ASKED QUESTIONS

Q. My major principal has issued me with visiting cards, describes me as his representative and generally avoids referring to me as an agent. He treats me as a paid representative. What should I do?

A. Use every opportunity to tell and show your customer that you are an independent agent. Your principal might not like it but, as he is not employing you, he will have to accept it. Failure to stress your independence will lead to difficulty in introducing other products to your existing customers.

Q. My new principal wishes to do a mail-shot to my existing customers. Do I give him a list?

A. You will both benefit from this operation so it is quite in order. Have no fear about using this customer information if you left him. Remember, these are your customers and it is your relationship with them that is the important factor. He is, to them, a third party. Also make sure that there are many names that you would like to be your customers on the list.

Q. My principal is refusing to continue dealing with a customer who is disputing an invoice. The customer is right. What do I do?

A. Diplomatically take the customers side without upsetting the principal. It will be a difficult task but a necessary one. Always be seen as acting as an intermediary.

CASE STUDIES.

Charles Gann found that, once he was selling again, he thoroughly enjoyed himself. As it had been a long time since he had spoken to his previous customers he did not feel embarrassed about approaching them and selling the products of his new agency.

He found that most of them were genuinely interested in what he was doing and readily agreed to see him and the product. He felt a lot of satisfaction when the majority of them gave him a trial order on his first visit. His principal rang him after the first month and stated how pleased he was.

Charles found great difficulty in portraying himself as an independent salesman. Due to his lifelong role as an employed salesman he slipped into referring to his principals company as 'we, us and ours'. The fact that the principal had furnished him with visiting cards with the company's logo on them and referring to Charles as their representative did not help. He decided he would print his own cards, describe himself as 'agent' and put the principals company name in the top corner, leaving room for other company names at a future date.

Dennis Wilson found that on the calls that he was able to make that he was met with a certain amount of hostility from some prospects. It seems that some of these people had already dealt with the company and had outstanding complaints that were, they said, being ignored.

Dennis took a note of the complaints and said he would take them up with the company. He then tried to sell them a new product from the company without success. He had not earned any commission on his first months' work.

He had a telephone call from the principal who wanted to meet him and discuss his lack of sales. They duly met and Dennis confronted him with the customer complaints. The principal told him he should be ignoring these complaints and that Dennis should be finding new prospects.

It was during this meeting that Dennis found out that they had started another agent on his territory.

Samantha Grey decided to use the computer to send out some mail-shots to prospects telling them of her appointment as an agent for the two companies, outlining the service she could give them and told them she would in contact in the near future.

The setting up took some days but she felt it would be worth it in the long run. She obtained the names and addresses from the local telephone directory and addressed the letter to the managing director in each case.

About three days after they should have received the mail-shot she telephoned each recipient and asked for an interview. Many of them told her that they had no use for what was on offer. Some said that they would like to see her and others said they were quite satisfied with their existing supplier. She made appointments with those who were interested and those who said they were satisfied with the existing suppliers.

She got the appointments with the latter by asking 'what would happen if your existing supplier let you down? Who would you go to?' Samantha was showing what an excellent saleswomen she was and how wise she was to have taken her career into her own hands.

Chapter 11

LOOKING AHEAD.

INCREASING THE GEOGRAPHICAL AREA.

This form of expansion has major benefits and major drawbacks. The chance to increase an area usually comes via a principal having an adjacent area vacant and asking you to cover that area.

the benefits are:

- you know the product sells
- you know how to sell the product
- profits from existing business

the drawbacks are:

- escalating travel expenses
- increasing travelling time
- fresh prospecting needed

If you are offered an increase in area by a principal think carefully and ask questions before you accept.

- why is the area vacant?
- is there undue competition?
- what existing business is there?
- is the arrangement permanent?
- is the area easy to reach?

As you have already learned, the less travelling time the more time spent selling. The addition of an area can actually decrease your profitability.

EXPANDING YOUR PRODUCT BASE.

This is probably the most used and profitable strategies used by sales agents to increase their business. The importance of taking on products that can be sold to your existing customer base must be stressed. It is also wise to take on complementary products or service. For example your credibility would probably suffer if you attempted to sell packaging machinery and life insurance to the same customer.

He would probably view you as an opportunist rather than an expert advisor on packaging machinery or insurance. Selling packaging machines and the materials that are used on them can be seen as a logical step.

The exception to expanding in your chosen market sector is where you have made a conscious decision to leave that sector. Such decisions must be thought out carefully before any move is made.

TAKING ON SUB-AGENTS.

With the level of commissions generally paid to sales agents, there is rarely enough margin to take on sub-agents and pay them a decent commission. Such arrangements rarely last long and can pose a threat to your relationship with your principal. Remember, you have no major control over a sub-agents activities and his actions could jeopardise your principals objectives.

If you do decide to go down this route to expansion, discuss this with the principals concerned and do make sure that the agreement you have with the sub-agent is written and in such terms as to protect your relationship with those principals.

EMPLOYING SALESPEOPLE YOURSELF.

Some sales agents find that they have created more business than they have time to handle. Others may feel that, due to age or physical limitations, they wish to take a less direct role in the business they have created.

This is when the question of employing salespeople crops up. This is a major step in the expansion of the business and the whole philosophy changes. An agent must realise that should he take this step he is losing his independence and that managing his employees will add an extra burden. The needs of his employees will dictate the direction of his business to a certain extent.

Most sales agents do not go down this route due to their overriding desire for independence. It mostly appeals to the younger agent whose desire, above all else, is to found a successful larger business.

TAKING ON OVERSEAS AGENCIES.

An extremely high proportion of sales agents act as agents to overseas companies. Many overseas companies wish to export to the UK and using sales agents is a logical first step for them. Many overseas companies may be looking for some form of stockholding so, in reality, are looking for distributors.

Nevertheless there are many good 'sales only' opportunities provided the product can be delivered from the principal in the time required. Many successful UK companies have started with a sales agency from an overseas company, progressed to a distributorship with financial help from the principal and then into a UK division of the principal with the UK directors holding a large stake.

places to look for overseas agencies:

- UK trade shows
- overseas trade shows
- commercial section of foreign embassies
- Agent Base
- local Chamber of Trade
- national newspapers

Possibly the best route is to go to trade shows either in the UK or abroad. Here the potential principle has set out his wares and you can assess many of the criteria we have already established, easily and quickly. It must be borne in mind that the principal is obviously on his 'best behaviour' at such shows and that a slick presentation cannot address such potential problems such as deliveries, creditworthiness etc.

Many innovative ideas do come from other countries but it must be remembered that innovation needs pioneering with its attendant financial risk. Do not be too impressed by a product or service that needs pioneering. This is not an area where a sales agent is at his best. Let others spend the money establishing the innovative product, you, as an agent, can possibly follow on after watching progress carefully. You will not make the fortune but there is rarely a fortune there. On the other hand your business will not fail due to the risks involved.

FREQUENTLY ASKED QUESTIONS

Q. I have been offered an addition to my area that has far more potential than my existing area. Should I automatically accept it?

A. You must evaluate the effects of the extra travelling, the extra time involved and the effect on your existing customers who are bringing you in your existing income.

Q. I have a son who has just left school and wants a job. Should I employ him?

A. There are many excellent agencies where the whole family is involved. Good principals applaud this because it offers them continuity. The downside is that it is hard to sack a member of your own family.

Q. I am a new agent and I am being offered an agency from overseas. Should I take it?

A. It would be preferable to have become established as an agent and learned the necessary skills first. Nevertheless, providing that you can cope with dealing with your principal in another country, there is no reason why not.

CASE STUDIES.

Charles Gann had spent several years gradually increasing his agencies turnover. He had taken on another three agencies and felt that the time had come when he wanted to expand his agency in order that he might start winding down his activities towards his retirement. He realised that he would need to either employ a younger salesperson or a sub-agent. He decided to employ a salesperson as he had more control over his or her activities.

He also realised that he needed at least one other agency to support the financial implications of employing someone. He had seen an imported product that fitted in with his product range. He made enquiries at his local Chamber of Trade, found the name and address of the foreign company and wrote to them. He wrote to them, enclosing his company profile in their own language using an interpreter suggested by the Chamber of Trade.

He received a telephone call from them and was pleased to find that they spoke perfect English. They invited him to visit them and discuss the possibilities of an agency.

During the flight, Charles thought back to the long time ago when he was worried about striking out on his own. He realised that with confidence in his own abilities, an ability to work hard and take disappointments in his stride he had entered the most enjoyable phase of his life.

not be concerned, either directly or indirectly, with the manufacture, sale or promotion of any goods which compete with, or are similar to, the products.

not give any promises, warranties, guarantees or representations other than those contained in the principals terms and conditions of sales.

give advance notice to the principal of potential orders to enable the principal to maintain adequate stocks of the product.

immediately pass any orders for the product to the principal.

comply with reasonable instructions from the principal

not appoint any other agent or sub agent without the principals approval.

Rights and Duties of the Principal.

The principal shall:

act dutifully and in good faith towards the agent.

at his own expense, supply the agent with such samples, catalogues, price lists and promotional material as are needed for the promotion of the product.

provide technical and sales support if and when reasonably required.

provide all Health and Safety information when required.

provide product training for the agent.

inform the agent of any order that he is refusing.

notify the agent of any expected lower level of business from existing customers.

have the right to extend or alter the product range after having given the agent reasonable notice of his intention so to do.

give the agent reasonable notice of any changes to the price of the product to enable the agent to conduct the sale of the product in an orderly manner.

Financial Provisions.

The principal shall pay a commission of .... on all orders of the products delivered and invoiced on the territory. (Except the agreed house accounts).

The commission payment will be made by the last day of the month following the month of invoice.

The agent shall forward an invoice for his commission based on copy invoices supplied by the principal at the end of the month of invoice.

Should the customer default on the payment of invoices, after a period of 120 days from the date of invoice, the principal has the right to deduct the commission payment for that invoice from future commission payments, provided the invoice still remains unpaid. The commission payment will be re-instated when the customer pays.

Confidentiality.

The agent shall use his best endeavors not to disclose any confidential information.

The agent shall not, for a period of six months after the termination of this contract, carry out any business similar to, or in competition with the products on the territory.

Duration and termination.

This agreement shall come into force on the date hereto and shall continue in force until either party terminates in writing giving the following notice:

> 1 months' notice during the first year.
>
> 2 months' notice on the commencement of the second year.
>
> 3 months' notice on the commencement of the third and subsequent years.

Either party shall be entitled to terminate this agreement if:

The other commits any breach of this agreement that is incapable of being remedied within 30 days of notice of the breach being given

An encumberer takes possession or a receiver is appointed over the assets of that other party.

That the other party is made bankrupt.

The other party ceases, or threatens to cease, to carry on in business.

Commission on Termination

On termination the agent shall be paid all commissions due to him under this agreement on the due date.

Should the principal terminate the agreement for any reason other than breach of this agreement by the agent, the agent shall be due compensation for the damage he suffers as a result of this termination.

Signed............ on behalf of.......................... Date..........................

Signed.............. on behalf of............................. Date................

Schedule 1   The Products

Schedule 2   The Territory

Schedule 3   House Accounts

USEFUL ADRESSES

AgentBase

Talisman House

11 Talisman Square

Kenilworth

Warwickshire

CV8 1JB,

Email: enquiries@agentbase.co.uk
Website: www.agentbase.co.uk (sample of magazine online)

Professional Sales Association: (part of Unite)

27 Old Gloucester St

London

WC1N 3AF

Tel: 020 846 27755